MEET THE S.C.S.

Greg Brittenh
coach for the New Yor
of Sport Elite Ltd., a cc .... atnletic performance. He written several books including **Complete Conditioning for Basketball,**and he also presented many lectures on
conditioning and jump improvement.

Vern Gambetta is president of Gambetta Sports Training
Systems. He has lectured on soccer speed and plyometric training at the National Soccer Coaches Association of America. He
has directed and produced a video on plyometrics entitle *Jump!
Jump! Jump!* He serves as conditioning consultant of the Tampa
Bay Mutiny of the MLS. Vern is available for clinics and consult-
ing by calling 1-800-671-4045.

Allen Hedrick, M.A., C.S.C.S., is assistant strength and
conditioning coach at the USAF Academy in Colorado Springs
and is responsible for the conditioning of the soccer team. He
has served as strength and conditioning coordinator at the Olym-
pic Training Center and has authored many articles nationwide
on conditioning.

Safe Plyometrics for Soccer Field and Goalie Play

TABLE OF CONTENTS

SOCCER PLAYERS' GUIDE TO *SAFE PLYOMETRICS*

B-I-A

Greg Brittenham, Strength and Conditioning Coach, New York Knicks
Following concepts of training specificity, the physical stress of training should use the predominant energy systems, movement patterns and sport skill fundamentals of competition soccer. Practice shooting to improve goal scoring. Lift weights to develop strength. Incorporate plyometric training to enhance the speed component of power.

HOW PLYOMETRICS WORK

Plyometric training enhances the contractile (shortening) properties of muscle and helps the neural component involved in muscular contraction. These principles are similar to stretching and releasing a rubber band. As the rubber band is stretched, energy is stored within the elastic properties of the rubber. When the tension is released, so is the stored energy, in an equal and opposite reaction. The greater the stretch on the rubber band the greater the potential for storage and release of energy. However, it's not the magnitude of the stretch but rather the *speed* of the stretch that ultimately generates greater muscular power. This stretch-shortening cycle is the primary physiological adaptation associated with plyometric training.

Jumping, hopping, throwing, striking and few fundamental movement patterns skipping, bounding, pushing are just a inherent to and enhanced by plyometric training. All movements involve a stretch-shortening cycle. In essence, plyometrics allow the athlete to "train" his or her neuromuscular system to react with maximal speed to the sudden lengthening of a muscle. Consequently, the ability is developed to generate a more forceful muscle contraction. With practice, this muscle contraction will be "timed" to match the release of the stored elastic energy, which is the aftereffect of the pre-stretch.

Another result of the pre-stretch is more muscle involvement. The more motor units stimulated, the greater the potential for power production. Sports such as soccer that require explosive, powerful movements can benefit from the principles associated with plyometric training.

The safe and appropriate implementation of plyometrics into a soccer player's existing technical, tactical and endurance programs are a valuable addition to developing strength, agility, coordination, speed, quickness, and, specifically, **power**.

HOW PLYOMETICS MAKE YOU BETTER

Power is the maximum force that can be generated in the least amount of time. Soccer is a **power/endurance** sport, combining strength and speed to enhance explosiveness, agility, coordination, and reaction/response time under fatigue.

Since strength *and* speed are components of power, increasing one while neglecting the other limits total power development. Unfortunately, many players focus on strength because they are familiar with this traditional and well-established mode of training. Because strength and speed both have an impact on power, athletes can make greater gains if they develop both components. For example, if an arbitrary strength score for an athlete was 2, and the athlete's speed score also was 2, the hypothetical power rating would be: $2 \times 2 = \underline{4.}$

Doubling strength without altering speed would double power: $4 \times 2 = \underline{8.}$

If the same athlete made only a 50% gain in strength and an equal gain in speed, the power rating would be: $3 \times 3 = \underline{9.}$

For maximum training benefit, therefore, soccer players should use a "total" approach toward athletic development.

It is important to realize that power development should be done separately from endurance development. The two should never be done together.

SAFETY CONSIDERATIONS BEFORE STARTING

✔ *The Young Athlete*: 🔋 Prepubescent athletes should be closely supervised. Because of their increased potential for joint injury (premature sealing of epiphysis/growth plate), young athletes should choose only those exercises classified as "low impact." The intensity, frequency and duration of plyometric training should be reduced.

✔ *Adequate Strength Base*: The athlete should have an adequate strength base before adding plyometrics to a training regimen. This will be determined largely through observation by the coach. An athlete exhibiting advanced physical maturity can endure training intensities above those of the athlete who has difficulty handling his or her body weight. *Plyometrics is by no means a replacement for a strength program.* Rather, it works with resistance training. Because power is the relationship between strength and speed, the stronger the athlete, the greater the potential for increased power development. As strength levels increase, the athlete may progress to drills of higher intensity and greater volume.

✔ *Intensity*: All athletes should approach a plyometric program with caution. Some drills appear simple and one might doubt their benefits. However, just because a drill looks easy does not mean significant physical adaptation is absent. The body adapts to progressive increases in stress. *Plyometrics should follow an intelligent progression, leading from less difficult to more advanced drills.*

✔ *Medical History*: Athletes who have a history of injuries or are recovering from an injury should not perform plyometrics. The athlete should resume plyometric training only with doctor or trainer approval.

SAFETY CONSIDERATION DURING PLYOMETRICS

✔ *Warm-up*: A complete and proper warm-up should precede any activity involving the demands of strength, power, speed, endurance and agility. An active warm-up should include jogging, calisthenics, strides, low intensity hopping and jumping, or other activities that elevate core body temperature. The active warm-up should be followed by a flexibility routine,

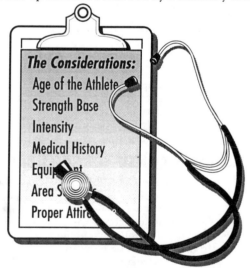

The Considerations:
Age of the Athlete
Strength Base
Intensity
Medical History
Equip___nt
Area S____
Proper Attir___

progressing from general to specific stretches.

✔ *Training Sequence*: Maximum neuromuscular adaptation will be achieved if plyometrics are performed when the athlete is fresh. Plyometrics should precede <u>all</u> other training activities on the day they are performed.

✔ *Progression*: The athlete should start with easier drills, moving to increased levels of difficulty when strength level and drill proficiency allow.

✔ *Spotting*: As the drills become more advanced, or as the athlete tires, at least one spotter should be present in case of a mishap. Athletes should correct spotting techniques when equipment such as boxes and barriers are used.

EQUIPMENT SAFETY

✔ *Surface*: All lower body plyometrics should be performed on a semi-resilient surface. Well groomed grass, rubberized tracks, tumbling mats, and artificial turf are excellent surfaces. The area should be dry, level, and free of obstructions.

✔ *Barriers*: Caution should be used when selecting plyometric barriers. A few unusual and potentially dangerous implements sometimes used by coaches as barriers include hurdles, tackling dummies, benches, rakes, shovels—even a rope tied between two American football goal posts. These barriers challenge the athlete, but are often unforgiving in a collision. Foam pads 1/2 inch thick and several feet long, "scored" down the center then folded to create a "peak" provide an extremely safe alternative to the traditional hurdle barrier. The height of the foam pads can vary from 6 to 36 inches. The foam pads compress (flatten out) if the athlete falls on them.

✔ *Boxes*: Box height can vary depending on the intensity of the drill and the ability of the athlete. Boxes range in height from 6 to 36 inches. They should be sturdy and padded (low nap carpet works best). The covering should be securely attached and not provide too much friction. The athlete must be free to pivot, glide, and jump on a surface that protects against severe impact but allows freedom of movement.

✔ *Footwear*: Shoes should always be worn. The shoe should provide a high degree of lateral stability, arch support, heel cushion, and a non-slip sole.

✔ *Medicine Balls*: Rubber-type medicine balls that *bounce or rebound* work best for plyometric training. The rubber gives the athlete more control. Weights ranging from 2 to 15 pounds will accommodate all ability levels.

PLYOMETRIC GUIDELINES

Adequate Strength Base: The athlete must have the strength to perform a drill *correctly* and without risk of injury. This is important not only for determining readiness for a beginning plyometric program, but also for assessing one's current strength base before implementing the next level of difficulty.

Warm-up/Cool-down: A comprehensive warm-up, flexibility, and cool-down session is highly recommended before and after a plyometric workout.

High Intensity Execution: Each repetition is performed with maximum effort. *Maximum force and minimum time.*

Fatigue Factor: Do not exercise beyond the point of moderate fatigue. Proper technique must be maintained to achieve maximal gain and decrease the risk of injury. A significant rest period between sets will allow best full recovery. Approaching a plyometric session "fresh" will provide best results. Even though a comprehensive weight training program should accompany plyometric training, the plyometric workout should precede the weight workout.

Workouts and Repetitions: A two- or three-day rest (48-hour minimum) between sessions will allow full recovery of the musculoskeletal system and further enhance adaptation. The number of repetitions and sets varies depending on the intensity of the drill. As a rule, a low intensity exercise requires more repetitions. An exercise with a higher degree of difficulty requires fewer repetitions. The athlete should not perform more than six high impact exercises during any *one* plyometric workout.

Exercise Difficulty: The beginning plyometrics enthusiast should "ease" into a program. Because many of the drills may seem easy or effortless, athletes may overextend themselves. It is not until the next morning, when they *roll* out of bed, that they realize the price paid for ignorance. Plyometrics are demanding and stressful, and a progression from beginning to advanced exercises should be followed. As a rule, the beginner builds a base by performing flat surfaced, double leg, and low impact drills. As a strength base is developed, more demanding exercises such as single leg work, barriers, and depth drops can be incorporated.

Evaluation: Every program that includes plyometrics should have a series of field tests. Such tests will establish a current baseline of athleticism, and can be used to assess quantitative changes, both positive (tangible increases as a result of training) or negative (decrements which may be the result of an injury). The nature of this testing allows the coach and athlete to draw conclusions concerning the effectiveness of one's training regimen. The test results also indicate individual strengths and weaknesses, providing a focus where training objectives are realized.

The Guidelines:

Adequate Strength
Warm-up/cool-downs
Execution
Fatigue
Workouts/reps
Difficulty
Evaluation

PLYOMETRICS FOR FIELD PLAY

Vern Gambetta, Soccer Conditioning Specialist (S.C.S), Optimum Sports Training

Soccer is a game of quick starts, quick stops, and rapid changes of direction. Plyometric training can figure significantly in specific preparation for those demands. The amount and type of plyometric work must be related to the training age of your players as well as to the length of practice and the amount of time players spend on their feet. If not used properly in relation to the demands of soccer, plyometric training can lead to injury.

PLYOMETRIC TRAINING AND THE DEMANDS OF SOCCER

Plyometric training is specific work for enhancing explosive power. It is a training method best used with other power development methods as part of a complete training program. Such a program improves the relationship between maximum strength and explosive power. In soccer, as in most athletic events, there is seldom enough time (.5 to .7 sec.) to develop maximum strength. The explosive/ballistic movements of soccer take only a fraction of that time. Plyometric training emphasizes generating the highest possible force in the shortest period of time, then controlling and utilizing this force to stop, change direction, or kick the ball.

DESIGNING YOUR PLYOMETRICS PROGRAM

Training Load

The prime consideration in plyometric training, as in any training method, is determining appropriate training loads. The following factors must be considered to determine training load:

Direction of Body Movement

Horizontal movement is less stressful than vertical movement.

This is dependent on the weight of the athlete and the technical ability in performing the jumps.

Weight of the Athlete

The heavier the athlete, the greater the training demand. A low demand in-place jump for a light athlete can be a high-demand jump for a heavy athlete.

Limb Involvement

Single-leg and arm exercises are of greater training demand than double support exercise. For example, single-leg repetitive hops are more stressful than repetitive double-leg jumps.

Speed of the execution of the exercise

Increased speed of execution on exercises like single-leg hops or alternate-leg bounding raises the training demand.

External load

Adding external load (such as a weight vest) significantly raises the training demand. Note that external loading slows the movement, thus negating some of the advantages of plyometric training.

Volume

The greater the volume of training, the higher the training demand. Essentially, training volume can be high if the intensity of the plyometric activity is low. As a rule, the younger the athlete is in terms of training age and stage of development, the lower the volume of plyometric activities.

Intensity

Greater intensity raises the training demand. It is important to remember, however, that the nature of plyometric exercises demands high intensity work for optimum return. The more advanced the athlete, the greater the tolerance for a volume of higher intensity work.

Density

Density is the number of times plyometric training is performed within a particular training cycle. The greater the density, the greater the training demand. As a general rule, no more than three plyometric sessions should be done in a seven-day workout cycle.

Training Age

Training age is the number of years an athlete has been in a formal training program. At younger training ages the overall training demand should be kept low. With beginners, it is possible to get a large number of contacts with minimum stress through game activities such as jump rope, jumping relays, etc.

Basic Strength

Conventional wisdom dictates that prerequisite strength levels are necessary before beginning plyometric training. Criteria such as the ability to squat two times body weight or leg press two and one-half times body weight are quite high and often unreasonable, especially for the soccer player who does not require these strength levels to play the game. Basic strength has two important considerations: stabilization strength (force generated for body control) and eccentric strength (force generated as muscles lengthen).

The prime concern when incorporating plyometric training in a program is strength in the stabilizing muscles, which prevents injury. The stabilization strength level can be determined by several simple tests, easily administered and easily interpreted If the athlete cannot satisfactorily perform these tests, then he or she should begin a remedial program of balance and stabilization exercises. These qualities should be brought up to acceptable standards before plyometrics are incorporated into the training program.

BALANCE AND STABILIZATION TESTS (KLATT 1988)

All tests are performed without shoes to test the stabilizers of the foot and ankle.

Static Stand (Hip Flexed)—Appropriate for use with all ages
a) Stand erect on one foot.
b) Flex the hip and bend the knee of the non-supporting leg.
c) Hold this position for 10 seconds.
d) Observe the ability to hold the position with as little shaking or lateral deviation as possible.

Single Leg Squat—Appropriate for use with all ages
a) Squat, bending at the ankle, knee, and hip.
b) Hold lowest possible position for 10 seconds.
c) Observe the depth of the squat and the ability to hold the position with as little shaking or lateral deviation as possible.

After stabilization strength, the concern is eccentric strength. Eccentric strength is a limiting factor, especially in more complex high-volume and high-intensity plyometric training. Without adequate levels of eccentric strength in the athlete, rapid switching from eccentric to concentric is difficult and inefficient.

Eccentric strength can be evaluated through stabilization jump tests and observation of basic jumping exercises. An excessively long amortization (lowering) phase and a slow switching from eccentric to concentric work indicate that eccentric strength levels are insufficient and the appropriate training should be remedial—low in volume and intensity. Before emphasizing plyometric training, the level of eccentric strength should be raised to an acceptable level.

STABILIZATION JUMP TESTS FOR ECCENTRIC STRENGTH (KLATT 1988)

Hop for Distance—Appropriate for use with all ages
   a) Hop maximum distance. Hold the landing (like a gymnastics landing) for 10 seconds.
   b) Compare the distance achieved with the right and left legs.
   c) Check the ability to hold the landing position for ten seconds.
   d) Check if the athlete lands bending at the ankle, knee, and hip, using all three joints.

Hop Down (off 12-inch box)—Use only with more mature athletes.
   a) Hop off the box for maximum distance. Hold the landing (like a gymnastics landing) for ten seconds.
   b) Compare the distance achieved with the right and left legs.
   c) Check the ability to hold the landing position for 10 seconds.
   d) Check if the athlete lands bending at the ankle, knee and hip using all three joints.

Repetitive Jump Test (maximum effort jumps)
   a) Jump repetitively with a maximum effort as rapidly as possible for 30 seconds.
   b) Observe how rapidly the athlete can switch from eccentric (down) to concentric (up). An excessively long switching time indicates a poor level of eccentric strength.
   c) Observe how much the athlete deviates from the original starting position. Deviation forward, backward, or laterally indicates poor balance and stabilization.
   d) Count the number of jumps.

Technique

Proper execution of the exercises must be continually stressed. The beginner, especially, should establish a sound technical base on which the higher intensity work is built. Jumping is a constant interchange between force production and force reduction, leading to a summation of forces utilizing the entire body: the hip, knee, ankle, trunk and arms. The timing and coordination of all body segments yield a positive ground reaction, resulting in a high rate of force production.

Landing is a key element in the execution of proper technique. The shock of landing is not absorbed exclusively with the foot; rather, it is a combination of the ankle, knee, and hip joints working together to absorb the shock of landing, then transferring that force. The proper utilization of all three joints allows the body to use the elasticity of the muscles to absorb the force of landing, then uses that force in the following movement.

This does not mean the fast strike is unimportant. By striking on the full foot, shock is absorbed. It is incorrect to land either completely on the heel or on the ball of the foot. This type of landing transfers high impact forces through the bone, the ankle, and knee joints rather than allowing the muscle to absorb the shock. The athlete should react to the ground as if the ground is hot, emphasizing quickness off the ground. A loud slapping noise on landing indicates that the landing technique is incorrect, and the exercise should stop.

The torso should remain upright, insuring proper projection of the center of mass and avoiding undue strain on the lower back. Correct postural alignment is directly related to core (torso) strength. If the athlete has problems holding the torso position during the movements, address the issue through a core strengthening program. This program should consist of exercises that strengthen the abdomen and the lower back muscles, as well as the rotational muscles of the trunk.

The arms contribute to balance and force production. Research shows that the arms can contribute up to 10 percent to the jump. They should be used to transfer momentum to the whole body through a correct blocking action. In my experience, torso position and the synchronization of the arms are the most difficult aspects of technique for the beginner to master. The Jumping Skill Checkpoint Guide is especially valuable when coupled with high speed video.

Jumping Skill Checkpoint Guide
◉ Posture
Head Position
Torso Position
◉ Foot Strike
Full Foot
Ball of Foot
Flat Foot
◉ Landing
Quiet
Loud/Slapping
◉ Leg Action
Amplitude
Synchronization
◉ Arm Action
Coordinated
Uncoordinated

Progression

A well-defined progression goes a long way to eliminating some of the inherent risk of plyometric training. Be cautious, mastering each step before proceeding to the next. Increasing difficulty levels can be done within each step, depending on the level of athlete and the ability for learning. Appropriate beginning activities include jump rope, hop-scotch, sack races, and various jumping and hopping relays that reinforce the natural movement patterns. Double-leg takeoffs are better than single-leg takeoffs at the beginning stages. Continually emphasize coordination, fluid movement, and reinforcement of correct technique, regardless of the step in the progression. The progression in teaching and training is as follows:

    1. Landing—The goal is teaching proper foot strike, use of the ankle/knee/hip to absorb shock, and correct body alignment. Begin with a simple standing long jump with a two-foot landing. This should be a sub-maximal jump emphasizing "sticking" the landing. Land quietly on a

full foot and absorb shock by bending the ankle, knee and hip. Repeat until comfortable, then hop out onto one foot. The objective is the same. Repeat until comfortable.

2. Stabilization Jumps—Reinforce correct landing technique and raise levels of eccentric and stabilization strength. Proceed as in the last step, the main difference being that the athlete now holds the landing position for a five count. Repeat until the athlete can stick and hold three hops on each leg for a five count.

3. Jumping up—Teaches the takeoff action and the use of the arms.
Start with a stable bench or box that is knee height. Jump up onto the bench. Emphasize a forceful swing of the arms to transfer momentum to the whole body. Progress to a box at mid-thigh height. Accomplish these first three steps within the first teaching or training session.

4. In-Place Bouncing Movements—Teaches quick reaction off the ground and vertical displacement of the center of gravity. Begin step four, which is the start of the second session, by reviewing the first three steps. This is a good warm-up and a review of the concepts. This step teaches an ankle bounce movement, essentially like jumping rope without the rope. Then, teach a tuck jump emphasizing quick reaction off the ground while bringing the knees to the chest. Keep the torso erect. Check to see if the athlete has the balance and body control to stay in one place. If not, do not move on. Also teach a scissors jump in this session to lead up to the cycling action of the legs that comes into play in the next step. This should be accomplished within the second session.

5. Short Jumps—Teaches horizontal displacement of the center of gravity.
Review the previous four steps. Start with three consecutive repeat standing long jumps (two-foot takeoff and landing), progressing to five repeat standing long jumps. Do the same thing up stairs, jumping onto every other stair.
Teach the single-leg hop. Work up to ten consecutive hops on each leg. Emphasize the cyclic action of both the hopping and the free leg. The action should resemble a single-leg run. Repeat this step for two workouts before progressing to the next step.

6. Long Jumps—Add more horizontal velocity. Teach alternate leg bounding and various combinations of hops and bounds carried out for 10 to 20 contacts. This is as far as most athletes should progress in the first year of training. The volume, intensity and complexity of the workouts may be increased by adding exercises and combinations of steps three through six.

7. Shock Jumps—High nervous system demand. This is an advanced form of training requiring a large training base. It probably has little application to the demands of soccer with the possible exception of the goal keeper. This consists of jumps off of boxes or rebound jumps over hurdles at mid-thigh height or higher. The training stress is high, so use this method judiciously. It is inappropriate for the beginner.

The exercises in steps one to six can easily be incorporated into a comprehensive soccer conditioning program. Plyometric training has tremendous potential as a training method for improving explosive power for soccer. Improperly introduced and taught; however, it is a high-risk, low-return training activity.

The following program overview is intended to give a broad picture of how all the components (Strength Training, Plyometric Training and Core Work) fit together relative to the level of development of the individual player [1 x , 2 x , and 3 x refer to the number of times that particular component should be trained in a week; following the overview is the specific plyometric program for each level].

PROGRAM OVERVIEW

Level	Objective	Off-season Training to Train	Pre-season	In-season* Competition
One **B**	Teach workout routine and correct jumping mechanics. Injury prevention program. Jr high school ages 12–14	Strength Training 2xBW Plyometric training-2x Core work - 4x	Strength training 2xBW Plyometric training-2x Core work - 4x	Strength training 1-2xBW Plyometric training-1x Core work - 2x
Two **II**	Reinforce correct jumping mechanics. Raise the volume of training. Increase complexity of exercises. High school ages 15–18	Strength Training 3xBW 1xER Plyometric training-3x Core work - 4x	Strength training 3xBW 1xER Plyometric training-2x Core work - 4x	Strength training 2xBW 1xER Plyometric training-1x Core work - 2-3x
Three **A**	Maintain the volume. Raise the intensity of training. Individualize the training program. College ages 18 & up	Strength training 2xBW 2xER Plyometric training-3x Core work - 4x	Strength training 2xBW 1xER Plyometric training-1x Core work - 4x	Strength training 1xBW 1xER Plyometric training-1x Core work - 3x

BW = Body Weight Exercises; ER = External resistance — essentially weight training.
*Frequency of games will be the determining factor in the distribution of work during this phase.

Each phase of the year has a general emphasis. The off-season is training to train. The pre-season is training to compete, consisting of bridging the gap between the more general work of the off-season and the highly specific work of the in-season. The in-season training emphasis is competition.

ⓑ - Level One
Junior High School - Ages 12-14

Off-season	Pre-season	In-season
Jump rope — 5 x 50 Jump and stick 5x5	Jump rope — 5 x 50 Jump and stick 5x5	Jump rope — 5 x 50 Jump and stick 5x5
Hop and stick 5x5 each leg Tuck jump 3x10	Hop and stick 5x5 each leg Tuck jump 3x10	Hop and stick 5x5 each leg Tuck jump 2x10
Lateral jumps 3x10 Tuck jump 3x10	Ice skater 3x10 Tuck jump 3x10	Zigzag bounds 2x10 Tuck jump 2x10
Lateral jumps 3x10 Squat jumps 3x10	Ice skater 3x10 Zigzag bounds 2x10	Zigzag bounds 2x10 180 Jumps 2x10
Vertical jump 1x10 180 jumps 2x10	Double leg jumps 3x10 Jump up 3x10	— —
Step close jumps 1x of 10	Double leg stadium jumps 3x10 180 Jumps 2x10	

𝕀 - Level Two
High School - Ages 15-18

Off-season	Pre-season	In-season
Jump rope — 10 x 50 Jump and stick 5x5	Jump rope — 10 x 50 Jump and stick 5x5	Jump rope — 8 x 50 Jump and stick 5x5
Hop and stick 5x5 each leg Tuck jump 3x10	Hop and stick 5x5 each leg Tuck jump 3x10	Hop and stick 5x5 each leg Tuck jump 2x10
Lateral jumps 5x10 Zigzag bounds 2x10	Lateral jumps 4x10 Zigzag bounds 2x10	Zigzag bounds 2x10 Squat jump 2x10
Jump-ups 3x10 Squat jumps 5x10	Jump ups 3x10 Squat jumps 4x10	Vertical jump 1x10 Hops 1x10
Vertical jump 3x10 Hops 3x10	Vertical jump 2x10 Hops 2x10	Rubber band jumps 2x10 —
Double-leg stadium jumps 3x10 Rubber band jumps 2x10	Double leg stadium jumps 3x10 Rubber band jumps 2x10	— —
Hurdle jump 2x10	Hurdle jump 2x10	—

𝔸 - Level Three
College - Ages 18+

Off-season	Pre-season	In-season
Jump rope — 5 sets of 50 Jump and stick 5x5	Jump rope — 10 x 50 Jump and stick 5x5	Jump rope — 8 x 50 Jump and stick 5x5 each leg
Hop and stick 5x5 each leg Tuck jump 3x10	Hop and stick 5x5 each leg Tuck jump 3x10	Tuck jump 2x10 Lateral jump 2x10
Lateral jumps 5x10 180 Jumps 3x10	Lateral jumps 4x10 180 Jumps 3x10	Vertical jump 1x10 Hops 1x10
Hops 3x10 Backward hop 2x10	Hops 2x10 Backward hop 2x10	Backward hop 1x10 Zigzag bounds 2x10
Zigzag bounds 2x10 Double-leg stadium 5x10	Zigzag bounds 2x10 Double-leg stadium 3x10	Rubber band jumps 2x10 —
Up and backs 5x10 Rubber band jumps 5x10	Rubber band jumps 3x10 Hurdle jump 3x10	— —
Hurdle jump 4x10	—	—

SAFE PLYOMETRICS FOR SOCCER FIELD AND GOALIE PLAY
from Performance Conditioning for Soccer

HOW-TO PLYOMETRIC EXERCISES

Jump Rope—5 sets of 50 jumps every day. To find the proper rope length stand on the middle of the rope; pull handles to reach under arm and adjust! Feet together, body straight, eyes straight ahead, arms close to sides, firm grip, rest rope loop at the calves. Jump with feet together just high enough to clear the rope. Jump lightly on the balls of the feet.

Skipping—Bend your right knee to a 90 degree angle while lifting your right leg waist high. At the same time, bend your elbows 90 degrees and lift the left hand chest high. As the right knee and left arm are lowered, lift the left knee and right arm into the same position. Emphasize speed and pushing off the big toe. (Fig 1)

High Skip—Emphasize height and extension of the ankle, knee and hip.

Fig 1

Jump and Stick It—Assume a one-quarter squat position, with your feet at shoulder-width. Drop the hips, swing the arms, and jump as far forward as possible, landing on two feet. Hold landing position for 5 counts.

Hop and Stick It—Stand on one foot, one-quarter squat position. Drop the hips, swing the arms, and hop in place, generating momentum with your ankle joints and extending your ankles through their full range of motion. Take off from one foot and land on one foot. Hold landing position for 5 counts; repeat with the other leg.

Fig 2

Tuck Jump—Stand with feet shoulder-width. Keep your body vertical, without bending at the hips. Jump in place off the ground while bringing the knees to the chest. Grasp the knees with the hands at the top position pulling the knees to the chest. Upon landing, immediately repeat the movement. (Fig 2)

Fig 3

Lateral Jumps—Stand with feet shoulder-width in one-quarter squat position. Drop the hips, swing the arms, jump laterally back and forth over a line, keeping the feet at shoulder-width and landing on both feet at the same time. (Fig. 3)

Ice Skater—Assume a standing position, with your feet shoulder-width apart. Jump laterally to the right, landing on the right foot. Immediately jump laterally to the left, landing on the left foot, jump side to side, pushing off one leg onto the other and repeat. (Fig. 4)

Fig 4

Exercise Day	M	T	W	T	F	S	M	T	W	T	F	S	M	T

SAFE PLYOMETRICS FOR SOCCER FIELD AND GOALIE PLAY
from Performance Conditioning for Soccer

Photocopy charts

Workout Chart

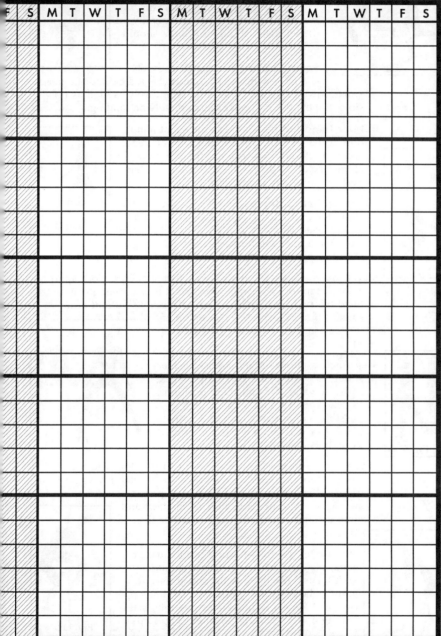

	S	M	T	W	T	F	S	M	T	W	T	F	S	M	T	W	T	F	S

Fig 5

Fig 6

Zig Zag Bound—Assume a standing position on right foot. Jump forward and laterally (to the left) off right foot. Land on left foot. Immediately on landing, jump forward and laterally to the left. The lateral movement should cover 24 to 42 inches. (Fig. 5)

Squat Jumps—Stand with your feet shoulder-width apart, hands clasped behind the head. Squat down to parallel and jump repetitively as high as possible. Repeat the movement immediately on landing.

Fig 7

Fig 8

Rubber Band Jumps—Same as the squat jump, only use a 48-inch rubber band with one end secured around the waist and the other anchored solidly. This provides resistance while performing squat jumps. (Fig. 6)

Standing Vertical Jump—Stand with your feet shoulder-width apart. Squat down to parallel and jump repetitively as high as possible using a double-arm swing for assistance, reaching as high has possible with maximum effort jumps. (Fig. 7)

Step Close Jumps—Stand with your feet shoulder-width apart. Take a step forward, squat down as if establishing position to head the ball, and jump as high as possible without arm swing for assistance. Use maximum effort and jump as high as possible. (Fig. 8)

Fig 9

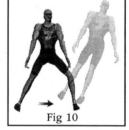

Fig 10

Step Back & Jump—Stand with your feet shoulder-width apart. Take a step back, squat down as if establishing position to head the ball, and jump as high as possible without arm swing for assistance. Use maximum effort and jump as high as possible. (Fig. 9)

Side Step & Jump—Stand with your feet shoulder-width apart. Take a step to one side, squat down as if establishing position to head the ball, and jump as high as possible without arm swing for assistance. Use maximum effort and jump as high as possible. Repeat other side. (Fig. 10)

Fig 11a

Fig 11b

Double-leg Jumps—Assume a one-quarter squat position, with your feet at shoulder-width. Drop the hips, swing the arms, and jump as far forward as possible, landing on two feet. Repeat as quickly as possible, maintaining correct starting position. (Fig. 11a)

Double-leg Stadium Jumps—Assume a standing position at the bottom of a set of stairs, with the feet at shoulder width and the hands placed behind the head or on the hips. Drop the hips slightly and jump quickly to the next step. Upon landing, immediately repeat the movement and advance to the next step. Depending on the level of the athlete and the size of the steps, the athlete should be able to jump two steps. (Fig. 11b)

180 Jumps—Jump in place, turning 180 degrees in the air, take off immediately while turning in the opposite direction.

Hops—Stand on one foot, one-quarter squat position. Drop the hips, swing the arms, and hop forward, generating momentum with your ankle joints and extending your ankles through their full range of motion. Take off from one foot and land on one foot. Repeat with the other leg. (Fig. 12a)

Fig 12a

Backward Hops—Same as hops, only travel backward.

Hurdle or Cone Jump -Assume a standing position. Drop the hips slightly, and, keeping the feet together and using a double-arm swing, jump over the first hurdle. Keep the feet together and the body upright over the hurdle. Upon landing, immediately repeat the movement over each of the hurdles. (Start with one hurdle set at 18 inches.) Once this be-

Fig 12b

comes easy, go to three hurdles placed about 6 feet apart, then go to five hurdles. Eventually work your way up to 10 hurdles. Gradually increase the height of the hurdles to 30 inches. (Fig. 12b)

PLYOMETRICS FOR GOALIE PLAY

Allen Hedrick, M.A., C.S.C.S.; Soccer Conditioning Specialist (S.C.S.); U.S. Air Force Academy

There are few activities where the relationship between a training mode and performance is as strong as it is between plyometric training and the goal keeper. Goalies must be quick, with an ability to change directions instantly. Great leaping ability is also a required asset. All of these attributes can be significantly improved through the use of plyometric training. Plyometrics have been described as the link between strength and speed. The purpose of plyometric training, then, is to utilize the increase in strength that occurs as a result of resistance training and transfer that to improved movement capabilities. What that means for the goalie is allowing fewer balls into the net.

PRESENT PLYOMETRIC EXERCISES SUITABLE FOR THE BEGINNING, INTERMEDIATE, AND ADVANCED GOAL KEEPER

It is important to remember that plyometric training should not be initiated until four to six weeks of resistance training have been completed, because a good level of strength is required to perform many of the plyometric exercises presented. Adequate strength levels are also important in avoiding injury as a result of participating in plyometric training.

Plyometric training should be progressive in nature, starting with lower intensity exercises and gradually progressing to high-intensity training. It is important that the athlete initiate plyometric training at an appropriate intensity level, based on the age and training background of the athlete.

Because of the high intensity of plyometrics, training should occur only twice per week, with at least 48 hours between training sessions. Plyometric training should be completed prior to other types of training, so that the athlete is in a non-fatigued state. This is especially true for the goalie, who rarely has to perform in a fatigued state. Because the emphasis is on quick, explosive movements, the keeper should rest a minimum of 1.5 to 2 minutes between sets and exercises.

For the beginning athlete, the key to prescribing plyometric exercises is to decrease the intensity and volume of training. The emphasis should be on correct technique, not absolute speed or strength development. Low-intensity plyometric training should consist of jumps off two feet with no added stimulus such as weighted vests. The exercises should primarily include activities such as jump rope exercises, light double-leg jumps, and easy jumps off two legs over obstacles 6 to 12 inches in height. The beginning athlete should perform three to four low intensity plyometric exercises per workout.

As the athlete advances to the intermediate level, exercise progression must be well organized if plyometric training is to be safe and effective. A sensible approach to exercise progression will go a long way in eliminating some of the inherent risks of plyometric training. It is critical that the athlete master each exercise before proceeding. The intermediate athlete can safely perform four low-to-moderate intensity plyometric exercises per workout.

For the advanced goalie, four to five plyometric exercises can be performed per workout. The emphasis on each repetition should be speed and explosiveness. The workout for the advanced goalie should consist primarily of intermediate and advanced exercises. However, beginning level exercises can also be used, especially as a warm-up for the higher intensity exercises.

For the advanced goalie, a good method to increase specificity is to use a soccer ball in many of the exercises. For example, instead of simply performing a drop jump, the goalie can perform a drop jump and then explode up and catch the ball at the highest possible point. This tends to add intensity to the exercises, because the athlete is attempting to get to the ball rather than just moving in space.

Tables 1, 3 and 5 include a partial list of goalie-specific plyometric exercises for the beginning, intermediate, and advanced athlete. Tables 2, 4, and 6 include example workouts based on this list of exercises.

Table 1. B- Beginning Level Goal Keeper Plyometric Drills

Two-feet Ankle Hop—The keeper should stand with the feet shoulder-width apart and the knees slightly flexed. Initiating the movement from the ankles only, the keeper hops as high as possible. As soon as the feet contact the ground the action is repeated as quickly as possible. Emphasize maximum height while reducing ground contact time. (Fig 13)

Fig 13

Single-foot Side-to-Side Ankle Hop—Place two cones, 6 to 12 inches in height, 3 to 4 feet apart. Standing next to the right cone on the right foot, the keeper should hop laterally to the left cone, landing on the left foot. As soon as the left foot contacts the ground, return as quickly as possible to the starting point, landing on the opposite foot. (Fig 14)

Fig 14

Side-to-Side Ankle Hop—This exercise is very similar the exercise just described. The primary difference is that the takeoff and landing occur on both feet, rather than a single foot. The goalie hops laterally 2 to 3 feet, generating the movement through the ankles. Upon landing, immediately change directions. The emphasis is on quick lateral movements while minimizing the time the feet spend on the ground. (Fig 15)

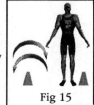

Fig 15

Fig 16

Standing Long Jump—The keeper should initiate the movement with the feet shoulder-width apart and the hips lowered into a jumping position. Using a big arm swing, flex the hips and jump forward as far as possible. (Fig 16)

Fig 17

Standing Jump-and-Reach—With the feet shoulder-width apart and the hips slightly flexed, the goalie should drop the hips into a jumping position and explode up as high as possible, touching a suspended object or a specific location on a wall. (Fig 17)

Front Cone Hops—Use 6 to 12-inch tall cones. Set six to 10 cones 3 to 5 feet apart. Set cones and 3 to 5 feet apart. The keeper stands facing the line of cones with the feet shoulder-width apart. Jump and land on two feet through the series of cones. The arms should be used to increase speed of movement. Emphasize reducing the time spent on the ground between each cone. (Fig 18)

Fig 18

Diagonal Cone Hops—Set a line of 6- to 12-inch cones 3 feet apart. The goalie faces the line of cones with the feet shoulder-width apart. Starting on the outside edge of the first cone, jump forward and laterally, landing on the inside edge of the second cone. Continue through the line of cones, alternating landing on the inside and outside edge of each cone. Jump and land off of both feet, using the arms to increase speed of movement and to maintain balance. (Fig 19)

Fig 20

Fig 19

Alternating Push-off—The keeper faces a box 6 to 12 inches high. One foot should be placed on the box so that the heel is touching the near edge of the box. Push off with the foot placed on the box, attempting to gain as much height as possible. The emphasis is on full extension at the hip, knee, and ankle. Upon landing, the feet should be reversed, so that the foot that was on the box is on the ground and the foot that was on the ground is now on top of the box. (Fig 20)

Single-leg Push-off—Standing behind a box 6 to 12 inches high the goalie places one foot on the ground and the other on the box, setting the heel on the near edge. Using the leg placed on the box, push off as high as possible. Full extension should occur at the hip, knee and ankle. Return

Fig 21

to the starting position and immediately push off again. The arms should be used to increase the height of the jump and to maintain balance. (Fig 21)

Lateral Step-up—The keeper stands beside a box 6 to 12 inches high. Placing the inside foot on the top of the box, push off with the leg on the box until the leg is fully extended, then return to the starting position. The leg on the ground is for balance only; all the pushing is performed with the opposite leg. (Fig 22)

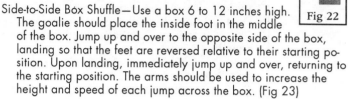

Fig 22

Side-to-Side Box Shuffle—Use a box 6 to 12 inches high. The goalie should place the inside foot in the middle of the box. Jump up and over to the opposite side of the box, landing so that the feet are reversed relative to their starting position. Upon landing, immediately jump up and over, returning to the starting position. The arms should be used to increase the height and speed of each jump across the box. (Fig 23)

Fig 23

Jump from Box—With the feet shoulder-width apart on top of a box 6 to 12 inches high, drop the hips into a jumping position and step off the box. Upon touching the floor immediately attempt to hold the landing position. (Fig 24)

Fig 25

Jump to Box—Standing in front of a box 6 to 12 inches high and 24 inches square, the keeper places the feet shoulder-width apart and drops into a jumping position. Jump onto the top of the box, using a double-arm swing to increase the speed of the jump. (Fig 25)

Fig 24

Step Jump-and-Reach—The keeper should take a step forward with the preferred leg, bring feet together, and quickly jump in an attempt to touch a suspended object or mark. Each jump should be of maximal height. (Fig 26)

Fig 26

Power Skipping—The keeper skips forward with an exaggerated knee lift, attempting to bring the knee to the chest. Alternate the movement between each leg and make each skip a maximal effort. (Fig 27)

Fig 27

Trunk Rotation—Sitting on the floor with the legs spread, the goalie places a medicine ball behind the back. Rotate to the right and pick up the ball, then rotate to the left and return the ball in the starting position. Continue for the required number of repetitions. (Fig 28)

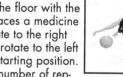

Fig 28

Some of these exercises may seem to lack specificity for the goal keeper. However, athletes at this age should have a variety of movement experiences. As the training age of the athlete increases, plyometric exercises should become more and more specific. Based on this list of exercises, example workouts for the beginning athlete can be developed *(Table 2).*

Athletes should perform workout A twice per week for three weeks before initiating workout B. Exercises from the list pro-

Table 2. B- Example Workouts for the Beginning Level Keeper	
Cycle:	Plyometric introduction
Goal:	Introduce athletes to the demands of plyometric training, emphasize correct technique
Length:	3 weeks
Rest:	1:30–2:00 between sets and exercises
Sets/Reps:	3x6

Workout A	Workout B
Single-foot Side-to-Side Ankle Hop	Two-foot Ankle Hop
Standing Long Jump	Diagonal Cone Hops
Step Jump-and-Reach	Trunk Rotation

vided in Table 1 should be alternated every three weeks for 8 to 12 months before consideration is given to advancing to the intermediate level. That decision should be based on how well the goalie is able to perform the beginning level exercises. Keepers demonstrating good technique should advance to a mixture of beginning and intermediate level exercises. Those having difficulty with the beginning level exercises should not advance until they are consistently able to demonstrate correct techniques. Goalies advancing to the intermediate level should select a mixture of exercises from those listed in Tables 1 and 3.

Table 3. I- Intermediate Level Goal Keeper Plyometric Drills

Fig 29

Split Squat Jump—Begin in a lunge position. Maintaining that position, the keeper jumps as high as possible. The arms should be used to assist in gaining maximal height. Landing in the same position, repeat the jump as quickly as possible. The front leg should be bent 90 degrees at both the hip and the knee. (Fig 29)

Standing Jump Over Barrier—Place a 12- to 14-inch cone or hurdle in front of the goalie. Bending only at the hips, the keep-er should jump up and over the barrier. Avoid turning the knees sideways or splitting the legs to clear the barrier. (Fig 30)

Fig 30

Standing Long Jump with Lateral Sprint—The keeper initiates the movement by standing in a jumping position. Using the arms to assist in the movement, jump forward as far as possible. Land with the feet in a parallel position. Upon landing, turn and sprint 5 yards. Alternate the direction of the sprint each repetition. (Fig 31)

Fig 31

Cone Hops with Change-of-Direction Sprint—Place a line of five cones, 12 to 14 inches in height, in front of the goalie. The cones should be spaced 2 to 3 feet apart. Hop through the series of cones, jumping and landing off of two feet. After jumping over the last cone quickly turn and sprint for 5 yards. Alternate directions of the sprint each repetition. (Fig 32)

5 cones and sprint

Fig 32

Lateral Cone Hops—Set up a line of four cones, 12 to 14 inches high. The cones should be lined up about 2 feet apart. Stand sideways at one end of the cones. The keeper jumps laterally over the series of cones, jumping and landing on two feet. After clearing the last cone, immediately change directions, returning to the starting point. Maintain a good athletic position throughout the exercise, emphasize coming off the ground as quickly as possible. (Fig 33)

Fig 33

Front Box Jump—Stand in front of a box 12 to 14 inches high, depending on ability. Dropping into a jumping position, quickly change directions, and explode up onto the box. The box should be a minimum of 24 inches square, so that the goalie has a large landing area. (Fig 34)

Fig 34

Lateral Box Jump—Stand lateral to a box 12 to 14 inches high, depending on ability. Drop into a jumping position, quickly change directions, and explode up laterally onto the box. The box should be a minimum of 24 inches square, so that the keeper has a large landing area. (Fig 35)

Fig 35

Depth Jump—Standing on top of a box 12 to 14 inches high, step off and land on two feet. Upon landing, drop into a jump position and immediately explode up as high as possible. It is important to minimize ground contact time and to jump as high as possible. (Fig 36)

Fig 36

Depth Jump to Prescribed Height—Set up two boxes, 12 to 14 inches high, 2 to 3 feet apart. The goalie stands on top of the first box, facing the second box. Stepping off the first box, land on two feet, quickly reverse directions and jump on top of the second box. The goal is to spend as little time as possible on the ground before jumping onto the second box. (Fig 37)

Fig 37

Side Throw—Have the keeper assume a standing position, with the feet shoulder-width apart. Holding a medicine ball, twist to the left, going through the full comfortable range of motion. Quickly changing directions, twist and throw to the right, attempting to throw the ball as far as possible. The ball may be thrown to a partner or against a solid wall. Perform for the required number of repetitions on both sides of the body. (Fig 38)

Fig 38

Slide Board (if available)—Stand on a slide board in an athletic stance. Vigorously pushing off with the outside foot, slide across to the opposite end of the board. It is important to maintain an athletic position (i.e., hips slightly flexed, back arched, head up) while sliding across the board. Keep both feet on the slide board at all times, and maintain a shoulder-width stance with the feet. (Fig 39)

Fig 39

Speed Cord Slide—Attach a speed cord around the waist of the goalie. The keeper should assume an athletic stance and slide laterally 3 to 5 yards (depending on the resistance the speed cord provides). Keep the shoulders square and the feet shoulder-width apart. (Fig 40)

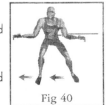

Fig 40

Speed Cord Vertical Jump—Attach a speed cord around the waist of the goalie. Moving against the resistance of the speed cord, the keeper should take two to three approach steps and jump vertically as high as possible, using the arms to gain height. Care must be given to assure that the goalie lands with the head up and the back arched. (Fig 41)

As can be seen, the intermediate level plyometric exercises have a higher degree of sport specificity. The intensity of the exercises is also increased. Both of these aspects reflect the training level of the keeper. Attention must be given to assure that the athlete is able to perform these more demanding exercises with correct technique. If the exercises are too advanced, they will not only be

Fig 41

ineffective at improving performance, but will also increase the risk of injury. Using the list of beginning and intermediate exercises, example workouts for the intermediate goalie can be cre-

Table 4. B- Example Workouts for the Intermediate Level Keeper	
Cycle:	Intermediate plyometrics
Goal:	Increase the intensity and specificity of plyometric training for the intermediate athlete
Length:	3 weeks
Rest:	1:30–2:00 between sets and exercises
Sets/Reps:3x8	

Workout A	Workout B
Front Cone Hops	Jump from Box
Lateral Cone Hops	Depth Jump
Side Throw	Speed Cord Slide
Slide Board	Speed Cord Vertical Jump

ated (Table 4).

Similar to recommendations for the beginning level, workout A should be completed twice per week for three weeks before switching to workout B. Continue to alternate exercises from Tables 1 and 3 every three weeks, to create new workouts. When selecting exercises emphasize variation so that some of the exercises require vertical movement and others lateral movement. Several months (18 to 24 minimum) should be spent at the intermediate level before introducing any advanced exercises. The goalie should be able to perform all of the intermediate exercises with high proficiency and also be participating in resistance training on a regular basis before consideration is given to moving on to the advanced level exercises (Table 5).

Table 5. A- Advanced Level Goal Keeper Plyometric Drills

Resisted Slide Board and Catch—Stand on a slide board in an athletic stance. Attach a speed cord around the waist of the goalie. A partner, standing just off the edge of the slide board nearest the keeper, holds the opposite end of the speed cord. The cord should be held so that there is enough slack that the athlete can slide across to the far edge, but tight enough that it provides slight resistance. Push off with the outside foot and slide across to the opposite end of the board against the resistance of the

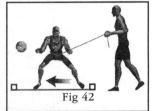
Fig 42

speed cord. It is important to maintain an athletic position (i.e., hips slightly flexed, back arched, head up) across the board. Keep both feet on the slide board at all times, and maintain a shoulder-width stance with the feet. As the goalie slides across the board a second partner kicks a soccer ball so that the athlete combines lateral movement and catching the ball. (Fig 42)

Assisted Slide Board and Catch—Stand on
a slide board in an athletic stance. Attach
a speed cord to the waist of the keeper. A
partner, standing just off the edge of the
slide board farthest from the keeper,
holds the opposite end of the speed cord
taut. The goalie pushes off with the out-

Fig 43

side foot and slides across to the opposite end of the board, toward where the partner is holding the cord. The speed cord
should pull the keeper at a slightly faster rate than what would
normally occur. It is important to maintain an athletic
position while sliding across the board. It is also important to keep
both feet on the slide board at all times, and to maintain a shoulder-width stance with the feet. As the goalie slides across the
board, a second partner kicks a soccer ball so that the keeper
combines lateral movement and catching
the ball. (Fig 43)

Speed Cord Lateral Slides and Catch—
Attach a speed cord around the waist of
the goalie. A partner holds the opposite
end of the cord, with enough slack to
allow the athlete to slide 5 to 7 yards

Fig 44

against the resistance of the cord. Maintaining an athletic position, quickly slide laterally. At the same time a second partner
kicks a soccer ball for the keeper to catch. (Fig 44)

Drop Jump with Lateral Slide and Catch—Drop off the edge of a
plyometric box, 15 to 18 inches in height; land in an athletic
position with the feet shoulder-width apart. Upon landing,
quickly slide laterally 5 to 7 yards and catch a soccer ball
thrown or kicked by a partner. Alternate directions of the slide
each repetition.

Drop Jump with Sprint and Catch—Drop off a plyometric box 16 to
20 inches high. Upon landing, immediately sprint forward 5 to
7 yards. A partner kicks a soccer ball, placed either directly at
the goalie, to either side, or above the head.

Standing Long Jump and Catch—The goalie performs a maximum
standing long jump. As the goalie lands, a partner throws a soccer ball. The ball can be placed either directly at the goalie, to
either side, or above the head.

Standing Long Jump to Sprint and Catch—The goalie performs a
maximum standing long jump, and immediately breaks into a
sprint on landing. After the goalie sprints 3 to 5 yards, a partner
kicks a soccer ball. The ball can be placed either directly at the
goalie, to either side, or above the head.

Standing Long Jump to Lateral Slide and Catch—Perform a maximal
standing long jump and immediately slide laterally 5 to 7 yards.
As the goalie slides laterally, a partner kicks a soccer ball. The
ball can be placed either directly at the goalie, to either side, or
above the head.

Cone Hops with Change of Direction Sprint and Catch—Set up a row of four to six cones, 16 to 20 inches high. The goalie hops through the cones, bringing the knees straight up. After hopping over the final cone the keeper alternates sprinting to the left or right. As the goalie breaks into a sprint, the partner kicks a soccer ball. The ball can be placed either directly at the goalie, to either side, or above the head

Lateral Cone Hops and Catch—Set up a row of three to four cones, 16 to 20 inches high. The keeper hops laterally through the row of cones, bringing the knees high and minimizing ground contact time. As the keeper hops laterally, a partner kicks a soccer ball. The ball should be placed so that the goalie can maintain lateral momentum. Upon clearing the final cone the keeper immediately changes direction. The partner should alternate kicking the ball as the keeper is moving to the left and the right.

Speed Cord Vertical Jump and Catch—Attach a speed cord around the waist of the goalie. Moving against the resistance of the speed cord, the keeper should take two to three approach steps and then jump vertically as high as possible, using the arms to gain height. Care must be given to assure that the goalie lands with the head up and the back arched to protect the back. A soccer ball should be kicked so that the goalie catches the ball at the highest point of the jump. (Fig 45)

Fig 45

Sprint with Change of Direction Slide and Catch—The keeper should sprint forward 5 yards. At the 5-yard mark, the keeper slides laterally 5 to 7 yards. As the goalie slides laterally, a partner kicks a soccer ball. The ball can be placed either directly at the goalie, to either side, or above the head. The keeper should alternate directions of the slide each repetition.

Table 6. B- Example Workouts for the Advanced Level Keeper	
Cycle: Advanced plyometrics	
Goal: Further increases in the intensity and specificity of plyometric training for the advanced keeper	
Length: 3 weeks	
Rest: 1:30–2:00 between sets and exercises	
Sets/Reps: 3x10 on each exercise	
Workout A	**Workout B**
Alternating push-off	Side to side ankle hop
Lateral box jumps	Standing jump over barrier
Assisted slide board and catch	Lateral cone hops and catch
Speed cord with vertical jump and catch	Drop jump with sprint and catch
Standing long jump and catch	Sprint with change of direction slide and catch

Using exercises from the list of Beginning, Intermediate and Advanced exercises, example plyometric workouts for the advanced keeper can be developed (Table 6).

Workout A should be completed twice per week for three weeks before switching to workout B. Continue to alternate exercises from Tables 1, 3, and 5 every three weeks to create new workouts. When selecting exercises emphasize variation so that some of the exercises require vertical movement and others lateral movement.

Performed with correct technique and intensity, and combined with resistance training, these exercises will have a positive effect on the performance level of the goal keeper. Just as importantly, the confidence level of the keeper will also rise. This combination produces a more effective goalie in the net. As with any type of training, these exercises must be performed consistently for maximum effectiveness, and improvement in performance will occur gradually over time.

B-I-A SAFE PLYOMETRIC TIPS

- Always prepare for each plyometric training session with a thorough, active warm-up.
- Always think quickly and explosively.
- Try to visualize soccer movement and apply to plyometrics.
- Plyometrics development must be done when fresh, at the start of practice and after an easy work day or a rest day.
- Allow adequate rest between exercises. Plyometrics is quality work, not quantity endurance work.
- In lower body plyometrics, use body weight as resistance. Adding external weight such as ankle weights and weighted vests is for highly trained athletes only, then recommended on only a very specialized basis.
- In jumping, larger athletes experience greater intensity because of their body weight.
- Jumping in sand, water and other such media will reduce the effects of plyometrics and should be strength/endurance work.
- Always pay special attention to landing mechanics. This is critical to injury prevention.
- Try and do exercises on the field—avoid concrete parking lots.
- Think of plyometrics in progression. Jumping on one leg is more stressful than jumping on two. Jumping off a 24-inch box is more stressful than off of an 18-inch box. Three sets of an exercise is more stressful than two.
- Use cross-training shoes rather than soccer shoes when possible.
- Practice correct technique at all times. Incorrect technique is an indication of fatigue, lack of strength, and/or exercises learned improperly.
- Adequate strength and sound basic technique are prerequisites for plyometric training.

More Soccer Conditioning Aids

Subscribe today to:

Learn more about conditioning for soccer from Soccer Conditioning Specialists around the world!

Subscribe today to Performance Conditioning Soccer!

This unique 12-page, seven-times-a-year newsletter is devoted to the proper conditioning of the soccer athlete at all levels of play. Informative and easy to use, it offers basic information on strength training, speed development, injury prevention and nutrition specific to soccer (SR 999).

(Order form on page 35)